THESE HANDS THAT HOLD THE WORLD

Books by Xyvah Okoye

THE GOD-SEEKER COLLECTION
Thy Will Be Done
Understanding Christianity
Chasing God
Show Me Your Glory
Why Christians go to Church

―――

God Seeker: The Complete Collection

⇐ ★ ⇒

EVENTS TO EMOTIONS COLLECTION
A Darker Shade of Light
When Hearts Run on Batteries

―――

These Hands That Hold The World

⇐ ★ ⇒

AGE OF THE ANATHEMA SERIES
Tainted
Branded

THE COMPLETE *EVENTS TO EMOTIONS* COLLECTION

THESE HANDS THAT HOLD THE WORLD

XYVAH OKOYE

Chartus.X

THESE HANDS THAT HOLD THE WORLD
Hardcover ISBN: 978-1-915129-16-1
Paperback ISBN: 978-1-915129-17-8

A darker shade of light copyright ©Xyvah Okoye, 2019
When hearts run on batteries copyright ©Xyvah Okoye, 2021
This omnibus edition published in 2023 by Chartus.X
www.chartusx.org

Proofed by Caitlin Miller
Images from canva.com

The moral right of Xyvah Okoye to be identified as the author of this work has been asserted in accordance with the Copyright, Designs and Patents Act of 1988.
All rights reserved under international copyright law.

This one is for the little girl who dreamed it and did it even when the world said she couldn't.

Trigger Warnings:
This book contains scenes of self-harm, suicide, sexual content.

Contents

1. Stop 1
2. Tissues 3

A DARKER SHADE OF LIGHT

3. Crumbling 7
4. A Thousand Times 9
5. Cuppa 12
6. Embrace 15
7. And I Am Left Tired 17
8. Even 20
9. You Couldn't See That 23
10. Scared 26
11. For The Last Time 28
12. Grandpa's Shoes 29
13. He Came Knocking 32
14. I Need You Now 35
15. I Stole His Books 36
16. In The Night 38
17. Locked Doors And Lost Keys 41
18. Over The Edge 45
19. Sonnet 47
20. The Mask 49
21. The Passenger 51

22. The Race 53
23. Things I'll Never Say 56
24. Words Make It Real 58
25. We March On 60

WHEN HEARTS RUN ON BATTERIES

26. Always Forever 65
27. Beautifully Broken 68
28. Between Two Worlds 70
29. Camouflage My Thoughts 72
30. Circle Of Life 74
31. Crimson Tears 77
32. Crossfire 80
33. Dear Pain 82
34. Forget Me Not 84
35. Grace, I Need 87
36. His Luxury Coupé 89
37. I Am Spent 92
38. I Cry 94
39. I Have Been Deceived 97
40. I Wish 100
41. If Love Is A Crime 104
42. I'm Learning To Love 106
43. I'm Fine 108
44. Just A Fact 110
45. Maybe 112

46. Mumbo Jumbo	114
47. Some days	116
48. Poetry In Motion	118
49. Puzzling Questions Of The Heart	119
50. Scars	121
51. Selfish	127
52. Step By Step	129
53. The Remedy	131
54. The Source	135
55. Undeserved Gratification	137
56. Will Not Be Taught	139
57. You And Me	140

Stop

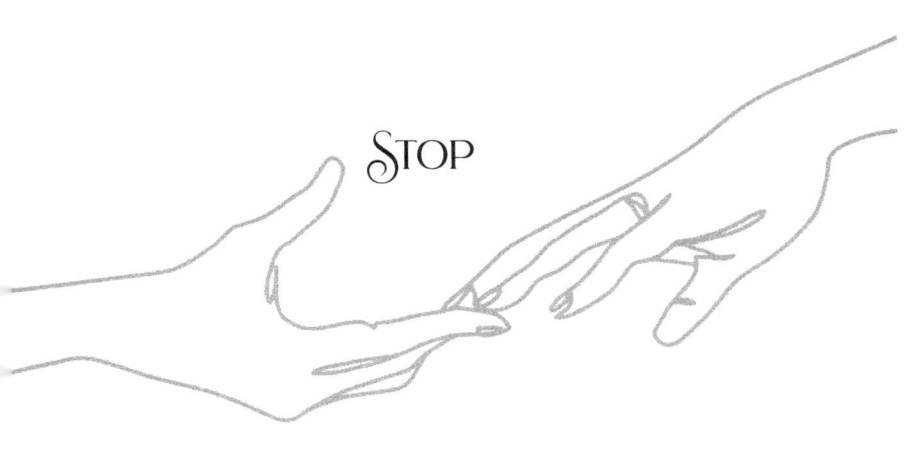

In a pick-up truck by the side of the road
Where my battery's up and my engine's cold
I spend the day out here, I need time on my own
I need time alone

Away from life, away from noise
Away from the sound of my own voice screaming,
"Stop. Girl, you need to chill out. Take it easy, or you'll
drop. Take a deep breath and just stop."
Just stop.

I hear my mama say, "You wage a war in your head

"and you can change the world, but you're no use if you're dead
"So get you out of your head, and take some time alone."

Away from life, away from noise
Away from the sound of my own voice screaming,
"Stop. Girl, you need to chill out. Take it easy or you'll drop. Take a deep breath and just stop."
Just stop.

Take some time today for a getaway
And when the voices say, "It's over,"
Remember, you still have the right to fight for another day
So don't you give up now cos you're a soldier.

Tissues

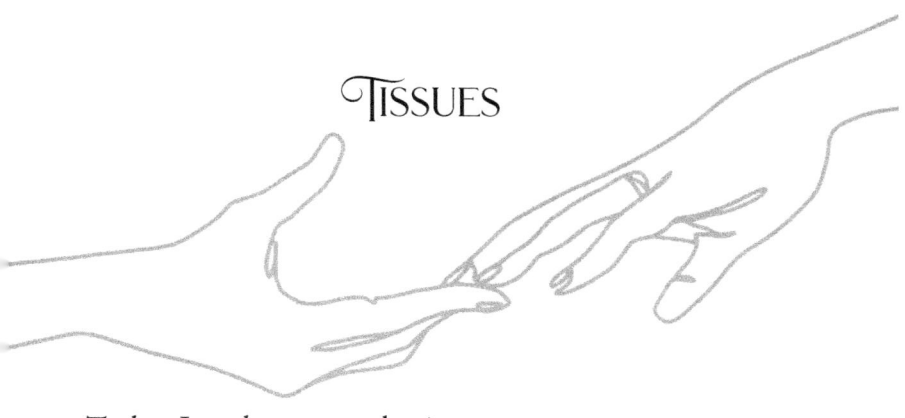

Today, I made sure to take tissues
Made sure to brush my hair and gloss my lips,
To blush my cheeks and smile.

Made sure to hide my tears behind lids laden with waterproof mascara
Because ruined makeup makes you a freak
Because freaks make people uncomfortable

Because the comfort of many is valued over the dying light of one.

It's considered fine—normal, even—to die silently inside
As long as you don't inconvenience those around you
As long as you don't make them feel uncomfortable.

So, today, I made sure to take tissues
Made sure to brush my hair and gloss my lips
To blush my cheeks and smile.

A Darker Shade of Light

CRUMBLING

I'm slowly falling apart
Slowly falling to pieces
As tears trickle down my smiling face
And the lies escape my lips;
"I'm fine... I'm okay... I walk in the strength of the Lord."

Because you cannot see the damage that's been done
You will never know how hard it was for me to give my heart to you
And I'll smile and laugh and act like I'm fine
To protect you
So you never know how hard it is to move on from you

But I love you
So, I will protect you
Shield you
From the destruction within me as my heart crumbles
like paper turned to ash by the flames of pain
I will protect you from the flames

And only my pillow will know how much I've cried
Only my bed will know how many times I needed to just be held
Only God will know how much it took for me to simply get up,
to just show up
Not to give up

But because I love you
I will protect you
So even if you ever read this
You will never even know it was because of you.

A Thousand Times

I feel the cold of the water as I sink in
Sliding down in the tub
I feel it filling my lungs,
Feel it burning, feel the pain
As I feel myself drowning
Over and over and over again

I feel the blade run across my skin
My steady grip on the knife
Steadily I press harder and harder
And watch the beads of blood break through
Running freely down my wrist

Just running, and running, until I run dry

I feel the pills in my hand, the little beady pills
Hard in my mouth as they go down my throat
One by one, two by two, till the whole bottle is empty
As I lie in bed, hoping to just fall asleep,
And sleep, and sleep, and never wake up

I feel the cool, clear liquid touch my lips
It burns, it burns as it slides down my throat
It burns as I take the first gulp, then the next
Till I finally drink the whole bottle
"It's purging me," I tell myself, "cleansing me from within, washing me, a stain on life, away from this world"
It burns, and burns, and burns, till I can feel no more.

I feel the cold iron so hard on my skin,
As I sit on the balcony railing
Wishing, and hoping, even praying for death,
I lean forward, look down below to the concrete pavement
As I watch the pavement rushing toward me
Rushing, and rushing, and rushing, till we finally collide

I feel the cloth so soft on my skin

As I tighten the noose around my neck
Silk, it was? or cotton, maybe? I could no longer tell
All I could feel was the hard chair underneath my feet
As I kicked it and fell, suspended in mid-air
Just hanging, and hanging, and hanging

And although words may die, memories don't
The memories of every harsh word they spoke
Of every mean tone they took, of every phone call they cut
I feel it all over again, like it was happening
Over and over and over again

And my heart starts bleeding, and my head starts spinning
And I hit the pavement, and I kick the chair,
And I down the pills, and I drink that s**t
And I press the blade, and I breathe in the water
And I die, over and over and over again

And though I die a thousand times each day,
My heart keeps beating,
The world keeps spinning
And life goes on.

Cuppa

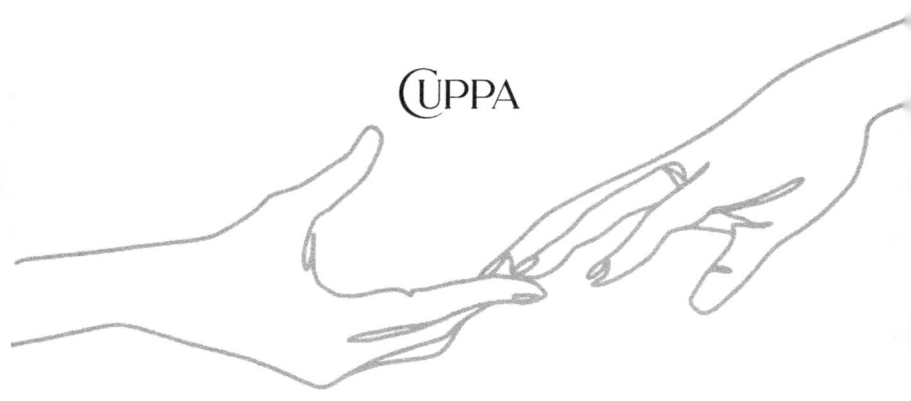

I stare outside my window, over the treetops, watching the branches sway gently in the morning breeze.

Perhaps I'll have a cuppa or two, some milk, three sugars, that should do. I'll put the teapot on to brew, but before I do, I stare outside my window, over the treetops, watching the branches sway gently in the midday breeze.

Let's get that cuppa, shall we? Maybe, have some biscuits too? Yes, some rich tea, digestives, or buttered crackers should do. I'll get some cheese spread from the fridge, but just before I do, I stare outside my window, over the treetops, watching the branches sway gently in the afternoon breeze.

Here now, about that cuppa, I think that I will bake, I'll use some cream or custard too, and have it all with cake. I smile and turn the oven on, but just before I do, I stare outside my window, over the treetops, watching the branches sway gently in the evening breeze.

It's getting late, I must confess, so let's get that cuppa brewed. Let's have it all, the biscuits, cake, and throw in some macaroons. I'll live it up, enjoy it now, for the day is almost done, I'll grab a plate and serve myself, but just before I do, I stare outside my window, over the treetops, watching the branches sway gently in the twilight breeze.

Hmm, by the time all my food is gone and my cuppa brews, I'll lie in bed and read a book, or maybe I'll read two. Let me fetch it from the bookshelf now, but just before I do, I stare outside my window, over the treetops, watching the branches sway gently in the late-night breeze.

Oh gosh, it's time to go to bed, but I haven't had my tea. The desired cake isn't even baked, and the book, nowhere near me. My macaroons and biscuits and the cheesy spread I craved have waited patiently for me to have my cuppa made. But I stare outside my window, over the treetops, watching the branches sway gently in the midnight breeze.

Perhaps tomorrow, I'll have a cuppa or two, some milk, three sugars, yes, tomorrow, that should do.

Embrace

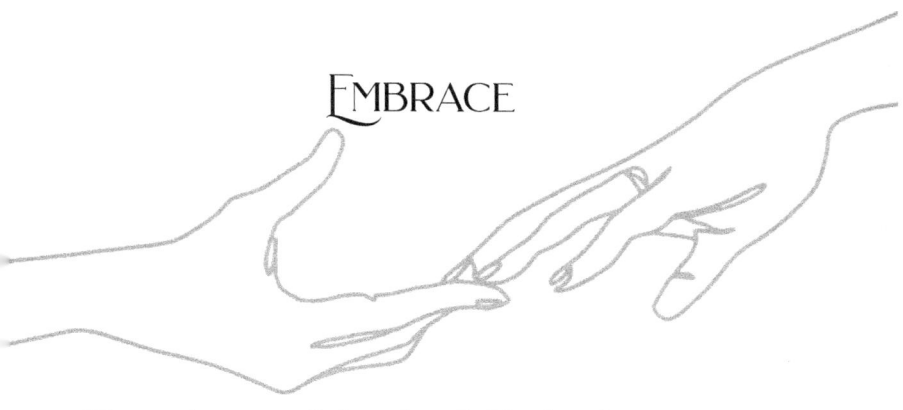

No words can quell the ache of a bleeding heart
As shadows dance on walls of empty corridors
The numbness sets in
As sensation is slowly lost to the alcohol running through my bloodstream.
This is how I cope with pain.
To run from it
To not feel it
To fear the overwhelming emotions that flood my senses.
That's when I realize, I'm afraid of pain.
I am afraid to embrace the ache.
I cannot deal with something I cannot face

And I cannot face my pain if I keep running from it.

And I Am Left Tired

Like my soul is slowly being sapped of the strength and will to live
My body, slowly becoming an empty shell of nothing but memories
Memories turning into bitterness and regret
Stirring up malice I never knew existed within me
The pain in my heart, once a constant burning, now a dull throb
Every feeling, desire, and passion, all fading away with the pain,
Leaving nothing but the dull echo of my pattering feet as I walk the empty corridors of a mind once full of dreams

Turning down the dusty hallway of a heart once bright and vibrant, once full of love
Now overrun with cobwebs and creatures of the night, now a safe haven for creeping things that dwell in darkness, now barren and empty of anything good, save the framed photos which hung lifeless on the walls, underneath a thick layer of dust, hidden well behind the vast webbing.
Pictures...
Memories...
Of times when this heart had once held life
Had once held hope
Had once fought for something more than just its own existence
Times when living hurt, but live, it did.
Times full of expectancy, of dreams, of faith
When the fight meant more than the victory and the claws of death were escaped by sheer power of will and the hand of God
When peace stayed the rugged determination to enact revenge and wisdom won over fury.
Times past, when life was for the living
Now, this old heart, nothing more than a throbbing sack of flesh, blood, and foul fluid, served the singular purpose of poisoning its bearer, of filling its living body with the

death it so longed for.

Slowly but surely the throbbing would stop, the pain would end, and that dusty old heart would beat no more.

Even

Even in the heartache
Even in the pain
Even in my doubt and fear
I choose to trust you.

Even as the light slowly fades from my eyes
And the hopes I had have come to die
And the thoughts swimming in my mind
Are drowning in the pool of despair I call faith
I choose to trust you.

I choose to believe that you love me

Even when my earth is shaking
Even as my heart is breaking
And my soul aches like it's never done before
And it will probably never do again.

Even as the tears I cry run dry
And the air in my lungs suffocates me
And the things I know are blinded by the things I choose to see
Even as I mourn the death of the person I knew as me
I choose to trust you.

And even as the sun sets on my joy
And rises on my pain
And the blood from broken skin and a torn-out heart bring no comfort like once before
And the one-off pain-killing pill only leaves me wanting more
I choose to trust you.

And although the light at the end of the tunnel grows dim
And my legs give in under the weight crushing my soul and killing me within
And the hole where my heart once was has bled me dry

And the tears that once held hope no longer fall when I cry

Even as I smile and go through my day
And perfect the art of looking ok with smiles and cocktails with friends
And although I know I won't make it to the end
Ending it all because I want it all to end
I choose to trust you.

So, in the turmoil
I will be still
And know that you are the one who saves
And even if you don't
I still choose to trust you.

You Couldn't See That

The message that midnight was clear

You were my only choice—and I was just an option.

But that didn't stop me from loving you.

It didn't stop the butterflies in my belly every time I see your face

Or the goosebumps on my skin whenever I hear your voice

The shivers I get at the thought of you touching me

It spreads over my skin,

My soft skin

As I feel your hands slide over it,

You kiss my neck and rest your cheek against mine

And I can't help but wonder,
Can you see me?
Can you really see me?

I wanted you to see me beyond the mask
So, I wiped off the makeup,
Beyond the clothes I let you take off
Beyond the skin I let you caress
Adrenaline swimming underneath it, to the tips of my fingers and toes curled up in tight fists gripping your shoulders as my thighs caress yours, all the way to the landing pads you chose to crash into as you pulled out your parachute, evasive maneuvers having me screaming your name like...
And yet I still couldn't help but wonder... Can you see me?
Can you really see me?

Beyond the skin I let you so easily invade
Giving you the privilege to be and do what others only dreamed of
Hoping that something within may open your eyes to see beyond my double-D cups and rounded soft butt,
beyond the smile that I wear on the lips I needed so badly for you to kiss

Beyond the hair that you pulled on which would not come off,
And the eyes that couldn't stop staring at you who saw right through me.

All the way to the parts I was scared anyone would see.
You saw the thoughts in my head play like movies when the words I said were muted by the fear of the truth...
Or the fear of the lie...
Or the fear of the fact that,
Although, to you, I was amazing in many ways,
I was still just an option—and you were still my only choice.
And although you could see me clearly,
You couldn't see that.

Scared

Sometimes it hurts
Other times it feels like nothing
And nothing feels like nothing
I know it gets worse before it gets better
But in a spiral of better and worse
Does it ever truly get better?
Can I ever truly be fixed?
Maybe I'm damaged
Broken beyond repair
Beyond the binding of broken bones
Beyond the scars of youthful encounters
Beyond the labels you were given

Which became more of an identity than the name you were called.

Can I ever... truly... be fixed?

Sometimes it hurts to be broken
To feel like a freak
Who can't even get their s**t together
Sometimes, I'm scared
I'm scared because I don't understand me
I don't understand how I feel
Or what goes on in my head
I'm scared because I can hurt me
Because I have hurt me
Because I will hurt me again
And if I can hurt me, then I can kill me.

For The Last Time

The crack echoed through the now empty halls
Bouncing off the walls of flesh and bone
Reverberating through me like a sad song stuck on repeat,
playing in my mind.
But only I could hear it
So only I knew...

And so. I said a silent prayer and vowed a solemn oath...
My heart would have loved for the last time
if it ever moved on from loving you.

Grandpa's Shoes

I sat upon the top step as Grandpa's things were shared
Like his house and shares and properties, his top hat, and his cane
I listened very quietly as the people spoke, and people heard, but nothing they said made sense to me because he was gone.
My eyes roamed from the crying faces to the familiar setting of the old living room I had grown up in.
His bookcases and hiding places, his chair, and then his shoes.
My eyes watered, and though I tried, I couldn't help but cry

Until I felt a ghostly presence and heard his voice reply:
"Don't look," he said, "to fill my shoes, those shoes were made for me. You have your call and life to live, so live it and be free.

"The things in life most valuable are impossible to see, like love, forgiveness, compassion, kindness, faith, and loyalty,

"So, bind them now around your neck, wear them for all to see, and one day, you would have ended up touching many lives like me.

"The simple things are still the best, like a hat, a cane, and shoes, so don't you worry about the rest, God supplies what you need to use.

"Don't cry, Ingor, you'll be ok, all these years I've watched you grow,

From ponytails to three book sales, you're stronger than you know.

"I've gone to be in a better place, to make sure your room is clean and tidy and just like you like, from the window, has a good scene.

"Don't try to fill my own big shoes, you have your own to wear, and one day, when you've run your race, you'll come and meet me here.

"You, blaze a trail and leave your mark, be who you're meant to be. And walk in my footsteps, not my shoes, those shoes were meant for me."

I woke up thinking, "Grandpa's shoes," I'll get them if I can, to remind me every day and night to live just like this man.

He Came Knocking

He knocked twice and didn't wait for a response before letting himself in.
Once again, I had forgotten to lock the door behind me. How could I have been so careless?
"I have a skeleton key," he said, "there's nothing you could have done to prevent me from getting in."

I frowned, a little put off by his brash and brazen attitude. An unwelcome guest was in my home with no respect, but he could care less what I thought as he made himself comfortable.
"There's nothing you can do, now that I'm here," he said,

"you'd better make yourself at ease."

He sat down, put up his feet, and asked for a cup of tea. Is he for real? I thought to myself as he casually dismissed me.

"I'll have what I want, whenever I want," he said, "so hop to it because there's nothing you can do about it."

Was this really happening? This unwanted stranger, breaking and entering, trespassing on my property and barking orders at me?

"Fetch me some biscuits while you're at it," he said, "I really need my strength today."

"And why should I worry what you want or need?" I asked, "I never invited you here."

"My dear," he said, "I need no invitation, I can go anywhere. I have the keys to every house, but today I stopped at yours. Don't worry, I'm not here for you but, to be honest, I'm looking for one of yours."

"No!" I cried, "you can't do that! I won't let you."

"I'm death," he laughed, "I can do what I want, and I don't need permission from you. Thank you for the tea, I'll take my leave, but before I do, though you treat me with hostility and do not want to accept me, I came cordially to you, so you would know me personally and after I am here and gone and everything is said and done, and you sit alone, questioning, wondering, do not beat yourself up but know in your heart, that though you tried your best, there was nothing you could do."

He turned in the doorway as he stepped out, "There was nothing you could do."
The door swung shut behind him and, this time, I remembered to lock it.

I Need You Now

I need you now

More than the air I breathe

More than the life I live

More than this broken heart that beats within me

I need you now.

I Stole His Books

I used to steal his books and hide them underneath the bed. Then, late at night, I'd get my torch or sit by the window, reading in the moonlight.

So many times, I'd go to sleep in the afternoon or pretend that I was ill so I could be alone, then I'd pull out my little book, stashed away in my safe hiding place, and read to my heart's content.

Then, in the middle of the night, I'd creep down the corridor, through the parlor and into his study, to return the precious object home.

I was stealthy, so I never got caught, there's no way he ever knew. I'd creep into his study, a paradise for me, a shrove of hidden treasures, worlds within a world, and I'd always find something to read.

My grandpa, you see, he read a lot, and my mama did too, so it was only natural for me to fall in love with the knowledge between the covers, hidden on the pages.

One day, I promised as I ran my finger across the neatly aligned spines on a shelf, I'll write a book one day, and he will read that too.

In The Night

In the night, you held my hand so tightly when you said you loved me
That night, you lay down beside me in my bed, and you showed me
The night it all began for me, my dreams and all my fantasies came true
I loved you
And that night I saw my destiny
I looked into your eyes, and then I knew.

We walked into the night
The stars were shining bright

The beauty of that night embraced the morning light
It led me to this place where all my dreams had now come true
Though I only dreamt of you until the morning light
We walked into the night.

In the night, you let my hand fall as you turned away, and I knew it that night
I could see it in your eyes what you would say if I let you
The night I now began to see that my dreams and all my fantasies were through
Though I loved you, that night I saw my destiny,
I looked through my eyes, and I could not find you.

So, you walked into the night
The stars were shining bright
The beauty of that night awaits the morning light
And leads me to this place where all my dreams do not come true
Though I only dream of you until the morning light
You walked into the night.

In the night, I wipe my tears as I can't fall asleep
I'm still thinking about you late at night
Cradle my broken heart as it begins to weep and pull

through

The daytime now gets really tough, so the darkness gives me rest and peace of mind

Because the nighttime tried, it did its best, though we couldn't stand to pass the test of time

But it should heal me as I walk into the night
When the stars are shining bright
The beauty of this night will erase the morning light
And lead me to a place where all my dreams can now come true
Though I will only dream of you
So, till the morning light
I'll walk into the night.

Locked Doors and Lost Keys

A locked door isn't just a locked door; it's another way of saying, "Leave me alone."
There's a kind of sadness you can get addicted to.
The kind that slowly caresses your heart, spreading through your veins, softly killing you.

It's a good kind of bad feeling.
More of an acquired taste, I'm told.
It grows on your heart like a toxic mold bred from a life dampened with tears falling onto a pillow as silent screams echo through the dark, empty hallways of a lonely heart

It grows, spreads, breeds
Feeding on blood bled from the bleeding parts of broken hearts, which no stitch from any surgeon or operation forgone proved successful
As gores soak up regret leaking from past mistakes... because a heart that breaks stays as broken as the words we speak stay spoken.

So as the days grow longer and the nights grow colder, the battle rages on as the heart grows old enough to retire but not serving long enough to receive a pension.
She leaves bereft of attention, she remembers him making mention of a convenient way to love with a broken heart
So, body young enough to fight for it but the heart too weak to nurture love, she abandoned the battle
Like a king without a crown, like a bride without a gown, she exits the ring... leaving an undeserved belt behind as he dealt the knockout punch shattering the glass cage which held the pieces of her broken heart, she realized she couldn't find it in her heart to bear the title of a "wife" as she found she had no heart for him to find.

The once empty cage now shards as the shattered glass slices through her skin while she tries to search within for more than just memories colored with blood and tainted with tears.

She searches for something she can't find in a place that will only remind her that she failed, that her heart is a failure

That every cut and every bruise she was dealt was a well-deserved reward for a failing heart. That she was lucky her cardiac was not arrested for transgressing, and the death sentence was a just penalty... so she decides to stay at home.

You can't hurt someone else when you're on your own... so the best remedy for living without a heart is to live alone. Building walls high up and a gate made of steel to prevent anyone her body would appeal to from coming in, to hear the silent screams echo through the dark hallways of a lonely heart as she watches the mold growing and spreading, dreading the day she hears another voice say those three words, "I love you..."

But she does...
Yet she doesn't respond because she won't be held responsible for bleeding hearts or broken bones that aren't her own, so she locks the door and throws away the key because that's the only way she can say, "Leave me alone" politely.

But he doesn't seem to understand that lending a helping hand to her is proven by more than just an outstretched friendly hand... He doesn't understand that the only way he will ever see the real her is to get through the gates of steel and, down on bended knee, tell her the story of how he got the master key from the One who made the lock...

But until then, as she sits silently listening to the tick-tock from her biological clock, she screams in her silence as she grows addicted to a sadness that slowly caresses her heart, spreading through her veins, and as the toxins begin to reach her brain··· she's dying... softly, so she hides away the pain behind the smile she now maintains, behind lies about locked doors and lost keys... hoping that maybe, quickly, one day, someone will find the remedy to a broken heart.

Over The Edge

One... step...
    Two... step...
        Three... step...
            Four... step...
                Five... Don't step.

I tell myself not to step as I stare over the edge
Staring down at the nothingness beneath my dangling foot
Oh, how much easier things would be with one more step
Just one more step, over the ledge, over the edge
A step into the unknown... but I know it all too well...

The race of my heart with the feeling of falling,
The rush of the pavement to greet me with warm, welcoming arms
And most of all, the feeling of freedom that comes with falling... just falling, knowing it would all be over soon...
One more step, and I would finally be free.
So, I smile.

>   Five... step.

Sonnet

In the end, life is like a sonnet
Full of rhythm and rhyme
Juxtapositions of silent sounds and screaming dumb men
Speaking mute words to deaf ears as blind men paint pictures of a future they see
While illiterate scholars read prophecies of greatness and success to the poor as the rich laugh on in their depression
Because, although money cannot buy happiness, it can buy the things that bring it.

Life is like poetry, structured or free-flowing, expressive

or spiritual, it too comes to an end and is afterwards
summarized for readers who can relate
Or for critics to pick out your mistakes.

The Mask

I've worn the mask for far too long
Can't even recognize myself in the mirror
I'm sitting here, wondering when the pain will be over
When will the smile I wear on the outside
Finally reflect what's going on on the inside?
But right now, you want to use me
And you need to cleanse me
So you're breaking away, peeling off this mask I wear
Breaking me apart, turning my insides out

Yes, I want to be used
But I guess I didn't count the cost

Because the cost of my yes is far greater than I anticipated.
So, I'm paying a price I didn't bargain for
And bleeding on the inside while smiling on the outside

Because for every melody played
They do not know the price I've paid
Because for every lifted hand,
It has cost me my mind
And for every tear that falls
It has cost me my soul
And for every voice that's lifted in worship
It has cost me my heart
Shattered and torn to pieces
My dreams, goals, and plans
All my hopes and ambitions
My desires and aspirations
This is the cost of the oil in my alabaster box

I may look like I have it together
But please don't judge me when I finally fall apart
Because I have nothing left to hold it together for
This is the cost of the oil in my alabaster box

The Passenger

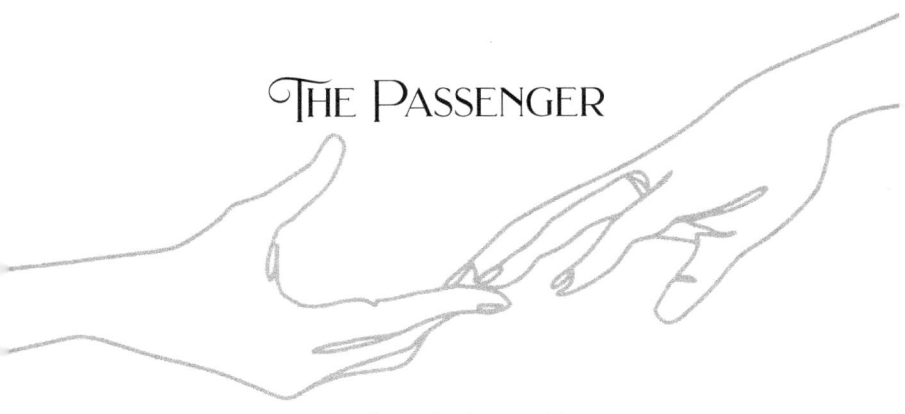

The rolling hills and valleys flash quickly across my vision
as I stare out the window
Watching my life pass me by
Like a passenger in my own body
I just watch

Through the joys and pains, the highs and lows
The good and the bad, the ups and the downs
I watch as my body moves through life,
Maneuvering around the obstacles in its path
Unable to assist, unable to engage, unable to truly
experience it for myself

I just watch, like a passenger in my own body.

The Race

From a boy playing football in the streets to learning woodwork in classrooms. Studying math, physics, biology, medicine.

Medicine, medicine, medical practices.
Now a man dodging bomb shells to catching babies, having babies, leaving babies behind. From a boy losing love to a man finding family, a new family begins, another baby is born, the man becomes a father, the baby becomes a boy.
Boys and girls grow from playing dress-up with dolls to make-up and curls, the girl is now a woman and the boy,

a man.

And as men and women meet and greet, mingle, fall in love, make love, have babies, a new generation begins as the woman becomes a mother, the man becomes a father, and the father, a Grand.
Now Nana and Grandpa, still mummy and daddy to their babies who are now men and women as the grandbabies become boys and girls.

And the girls grow into women, and the boys, to men, and the men meet women, and the cycle begins again. Another lap, another leg, another stretch in the race. And after a woman makes the boy into a man, again, another love, another life, another baby with another wife. And the baby becomes the boy who will one day become the man, for the man is now the father and his mother, the new Nan, and though Nana and Grandpa are still mummy and daddy, they are the Greats of the Grands, for they hold in their hands the baton of life as they jump the hurdles, moving the mark and making the way for those who follow.

They are Grand, for they go where others have not been, and they see what others have not seen. They fight so others would not. They walk so we can run, jump so we can fly, lead so we can follow, and even laugh and be strong so we can fall apart and cry. They are the Greats and always will be even after they are gone.

They remain the Greats and the Grands and the mummies and the daddies, no longer the boys and girls, but still the men and women who carve a legacy as they walk this earth for as long as they do.

Until they do not...

... and just like that, the baton is passed, the next generation takes over, and the race goes on.

Things I'll Never Say

I look into your eyes and I'm falling for days
The thought of the things I want to do with you makes me blush
And for a moment, I want to lose my home training
Just hearing your voice sends a tingle running over my skin
Electric currents for days, stirring up something deep within
Something I know I shouldn't stir up until it's time.
I think of you, and I lose my breath
Butterflies flutter about in my belly, and my heart skips a beat.

You make me feel like I'm fifteen again, without a care in the world and all the time to spend daydreaming of a life with you

Giving me a renewed hope that fairytale dreams do come true

I dream about the life I want to have with you

A home and a baby, maybe two, while you travel the world and I wait for you

The things I wish would someday come true

But I know, if I want something to last forever, I must take my time,

So I won't rush or be in a hurry, I'll patiently wait here until you're ready,

But all these are things I'll never tell you.

Words Make It Real

And once again, the sour taste of death saturates my taste buds as the words roll around in my mouth, on the tip of my tongue as I try to speak, but somehow remain unspoken...

Unspoken, for to speak creates a reality of the dream, the nightmare, playing before my eyes as I watch, detached, displacing the pain that bleeds through the cracks of my breaking heart.

Through the cracks borne, worn from use as a safety deposit box, internalizing my thoughts and emotions, waiting for the pennies you would pay to retrieve them from my mind, the piggy bank, banking the words that

now can never again be spoken to you...
Because you're gone, and all the things left unsaid, and undone, are playing in my head, my very own string quartet No. 14, as my 14th glass numbs my senses and loosens my tongue just enough to utter the words...

We March On

The darkness of the past is a sign of hope of a brighter future, for in the darkness, that is where the light shines brightest.

And no matter how deep the darkness gets, no matter how long the night goes on, we choose to believe that the day will come, the sun will rise, and we will smile once more.

With this hope we march on, braving the darkness and confronting the evil within us, choosing to believe that there is a greater purpose for our pain, that there is a deeper meaning to the darkness of our past, remembering that we are but mortal men with an immortal hope and an unfathomable destiny...

··· And to this destiny, we march on.

When Hearts Run on Batteries

Always Forever

When love is lost and hope ends,
And the tragedy sends volts of pain from your heart to your brain, incapacitating you
That's when you know your heart is broken.

When the million words can't bind the million pieces you can't seem to find as your cardia erupted,
Volcanic regret like lava leaking down your soul till time leaves only ashes cocooned by loss.

So, the sun smites you not by day nor the moon by night because you retreat to inhabit a steel house made of four plain walls that will not be blown down by empty promises and false declarations of "Forever Love."

Too scared to let in the light that once led you to the lover who tore your world apart when you still believed in having a heart...
In love...
In hope...

Hoping against hope that, against all odds, you'll defeat the enemy battling for your soul, all the while wondering what profit it would be to give it all up and gain the world
After all, all that's left is ashes
But from ashes to ashes, from dust to flames, like a Phoenix you rise again to laugh, to love, to cry.

And though you feel the ache inside, you hide the pain behind vodka and sex games.
Too ashamed to admit to yourself that you got played, you master the game, enslaving the world as the world became your playground and power became the aim,
You became a slave to your senses
All in a bid to avoid the pain of a broken heart.

But back to the start
To the one with the broken heart and the burnt-out soul.
To the one who almost lost their mind when the enemy stole the little hope in the heart that lit up the part of life that ever meant anything.
To the one step forward, three steps back
Stepping on glass like steppingstones, wanting to feel pain—
No. To feel...
Alone, knowing all along that it isn't the "Forever Love" lost forever that causes the worst pain...
It's the now in the "always forever" that never came.

Beautifully Broken

Raindrops dripping down the window, mirroring the tears running down her cheek,
A race down gravity lane, with no winner and all none the wiser, as the pieces of her broken heart hit the ground in first place.

Tears like blood outline the smile spread sweetly across her pained face
As she begins to comprehend the beauty behind the brokenness,
the bliss beyond the pain.

The loss hurt, but the love was worth it
And now, learning to let go, she smiles with gratitude for the broken-hearted girl reflected in the window.
Because, although the raindrops caress her oblivious reflection, she is aware of the truth:
She may have lost a lover, but she never lost love.

Between Two Worlds

Trapped between two worlds…
I cannot go forward
But I cannot go back to who I've been

The path ahead is broad and inviting
I need only take one step
And I'm carried all the way
The path behind, the straight and narrow
Holds trails of my blood, dripping
As I have walked it all this time.

The path set before me, the one I need take,

Is the path I am supposed to have left behind.
The path left behind me, the one I must take,
Is the path I am supposed to leave behind

 "Never look back! Never go back!"
I learnt on the path I now leave behind,
So how then am I to go back?
To look back at what was?
To follow again the straight and narrow,
When it's the path I leave behind?

I'm still pressing on the upward way
And my way has led me here.
Do I walk on forward to the broad-way future?
Or do I turn back? Retreat? Surrender?
Retrace my blood-trailed steps
To live out my future in the past?

I am trapped between two worlds...
I cannot go forward
But I cannot go back to who I've been.

Camouflage My Thoughts

I hear the bombs exploding,
The screams of men and women around me,
The unfortunate lives ended by one wrong step.

Arms and legs blown off
After all, if your arm causes you to sin…
And then again,
The screams grow louder, the fire burns, the smell of blood and burning flesh fills my lungs,
I need to escape.

No one can rescue me.

I need freedom from the catastrophe around me.
So, I open my eyes,
Drown my senses with a mix of one part vodka and two parts pills,
Hoping it will be enough to distract me from the war going on inside my head.

Circle Of Life

All reactions are to actions
And all actions cause reactions
All words can build or break
All wounds can mend or make

All friends have something in common
And being uncommon is something in common
All people tend to make friends
And all friends tend to make people

All pains cause hurt
And all hurts cause pain

All wounds may let out blood
And all blood lets out remains

Every sound breaks a silence
Every silence, too, breaks a sound
And every song comes from the heart
As the heart is inspired in every song

The fun in life is made by you
And so also, the fun makes you
The wrong always has something right
So as there is always wrong in right.

The master mostly teaches the pupil
But it's the pupil who teaches him to teach
The lawyer does defend his client
But the client has to defend him too

There's a law that pulls things down
That same law makes things go round
If you roll a boulder from Chicago
It will come back to Chicago

A circle has no beginning or end
For the beginning is the end

Our human nature and nature's miracle
Shows us truly that life is a circle.

CRIMSON TEARS

As beads of blood bleeding red run down my arm,
The arm of flesh has failed me once again.

And once again I am left alone
Alone with my thoughts, contemplating the complexities
of a simple word… No.

Knowing that the truth was all a lie, I lie here listening to
the sound of my own heart's arrhythmical beating as the
blood it pumps pours out through emotional gashes
across my left breast.

Gashes that only I can see and feel, invisible enough to conceal with a smile
So, I smile.

Even when it hurts, I smile.
Even when I can't breathe, I smile.
Even when my world is falling apart, I smile.
Even as the life drains from my body, I smile.

Because a simple smile conceals the myriad of emotions which flood me,
Like the calm sea with its deadly undercurrents, I am currently drowning in my own pain, with no lifeline or rescue boat. So, I smile.
Knowing that the only escape from my predicament is a permanent solution.
And though some may think it's a temporary problem...

"... The sea is calm today..."
The sea is never calm
She just looks calm sometimes
Her raging currents can wreck ships and drown men
But she knows that, as terrifying as she may be,
People are always attracted to a smile.
And so, she smiles

Beckoning both the simpleton and the adventurer to come unto her
Welcoming them with open arms
Leading them to believe that the turmoil they once saw was a temporary problem...
But be not deceived
Like the raging sea, I smile.

And as I lie here staring at the beads of blood like crimson tears running down my arm
I realize that it would have been okay to cry sometimes.

CROSSFIRE

Love is like a bed of roses
Even roses have their thorns
But I can't breathe without you
And even though time proposes
That I forget you and move on
I just can't breathe without you
We fight, then we break up
We kiss, and we make up
Is this going to be the life that I lead?
Would I cry? Would I bleed?
Would I let my children ever see?

Shotgun fires
I hear voices screaming,
Coming from downstairs
I'm behind the door.
I scan the room and look for shelter
As the bombs begin exploding in my head
Laying on the floor
Somehow, I've been damaged in the crossfire.

Love is not a bed of roses
As every rose must have its thorn
I'll learn to breathe without you
And even as time proposes,
I will forget you and move on
And learn to breathe without you
We fight, then we break up
No kiss, and no make up
This will never be the life that I lead
I won't cry, I won't bleed
or let my children become me.

Dear Pain

Dear Pain,
My old familiar friend
Despite the hunger and thirst for your company
I have decided to let you go
I have decided to move on
To get on with my life.
It's not like I don't want you anymore
You've been a faithful friend
Sticking closer than a brother
You've been there for me
Through the hard times
through the lonely nights

And the tears flooding my pillow
You've stood by me
Stuck with me
Seen me through it all
I feel like a traitor
For you've been my only true friend
But I know, where I go, you cannot come
And where you are, I cannot remain
So, we will have to go our separate ways.

Forget Me Not

Time changes, things change, people change
As we all head off in our different directions,
I lay at your feet
My one, final, and only request...
Forget me not.

Forget me not as you go along your way
As the places change and the strange faces become familiar.
As the things we once did become history
And the life we once lived becomes a memory.
Please, forget me not.

Forget me not as you go along your way
As the pressures of life begin to weigh heavy on your shoulders
And the things that brought you joy are far
And the time you have is well spent on surviving
Please, forget me not.

Forget me not as you go along your way
And the distance shreds my heart, tearing us apart.
Your face remains etched in my brain
As though the first thing I saw this morning
Please, forget me not.

Forget me not as you go along your way
And the healer called time cannot seem to mend my broken heart
As you hold me in your arms all night
Waking up to the bitter reality of your absence
Please, forget me not.

Don't forget the time we spent
The laughs we had
The love we shared.
I know I can't compare

To what she is to you
But if what we had was ever true
Please, forget me not ... I beg of you.

Grace, I Need

To believe your word is true
And to believe Lord, there is nothing you can't do
To believe you're on my side
And to believe that through the storms,
You will hide me in your arms

And give me faith to believe and the courage to receive the grace I need
Your grace I need
Give me hope to confess your will and nothing less than grace I need
Your grace I need

Give me courage to confess
That you want the best for me and nothing less
Help me see your will is better than my plans
Help me understand the things you do and open up my fisted hands.

His Luxury Coupé

Drunk on my sorrow, high on my pain
With so much to lose and still nothing to gain
Yet I drown in the chaos I call my life
Still believing the man who practically destroyed my life;

Who took a knife to my heart, daggered me with words,
With songs of love, of the birds and the bees
I didn't see beyond the signs, didn't read between the lines
The truth written in plain ink, though he refused to sign

I made it my mission, made him my world

Between walks in the park and kisses in the dark
From gazing at the stars so late into the night
He built castles in my head and a moat around my heart
He locked me in a tower and promised I was his
His good girl, he said, his special little girl
A friend he would never want to lose, he said
The one he wanted to be with, he said
The one who made him happy, he said
Yes, he said, no, he said, please, he said, I'm not letting you go, he said

No, he said, yes, she said, why, he said, no, she said, yes, he said
Roles reversed, down in the sheets, the bed soaked wet,
I bet you didn't expect that, he said
No, she chuckled.
Did you like that? he said, yes, she said
But it hurt, she said... But she didn't say, it hurt

It hurt like daggers pierced through her heart,
Like acid poured on her soul
To know she had been used and abused by the love of her life
To know she would never again feel complete
Never again feel whole

For she had given herself away
To someone who would never treasure her
Someone who would never love her

Someone whose heart was made of ice
Whose soul was carved from wood
Whose will was forged in steel
Who had used her to satisfy his raging desires
And held nothing but contempt for her now that he was through.

His luxury coupe, he called her
Now, the other girl, was her name
The face he once loved to hold, to kiss, to stroke,
He now looked at with hate and disdain
And then she asked herself, why go on?
Why go on living? She gave him her love, gave him her all
And now she's nothing but an empty shell,

So, she drinks up her sorrows and rolls up her pain
She lights it with her future and watches it all burn
As she drowns herself in a pool of blood
Bleeding from her broken heart.

I Am Spent

I'm spent.
I don't know how, I don't know why
I don't know where, I don't know when
I just know that I'm spent.

Pouring out my precious ointment
Washing the feet of the one that I love
The one that has no love in his heart for me
I'm spent

Washing his feet with all that's within me
He disregards the tears I cry, my crowning glory,

I lay as a rag to wipe his feet dry
I'm spent

Sitting at his feet to entreat his wisdom
He broods over Martha and her selfish matters
Though I give up my time to be in his presence
I'm spent

My energy poured out as I run to the garden
Still seeking him, though now a lifeless body,
He longs for the ones that mean more to him than me
I am spent.

Spent my body, that he may adore
Spent my mind to give him more
Spent my heart out on the floor
I am left with nothing more

All for love, I'm spent and sore
Once a prize, of glory, of awe
I now lay empty, lost, and spent
I am spent...

I am no more.

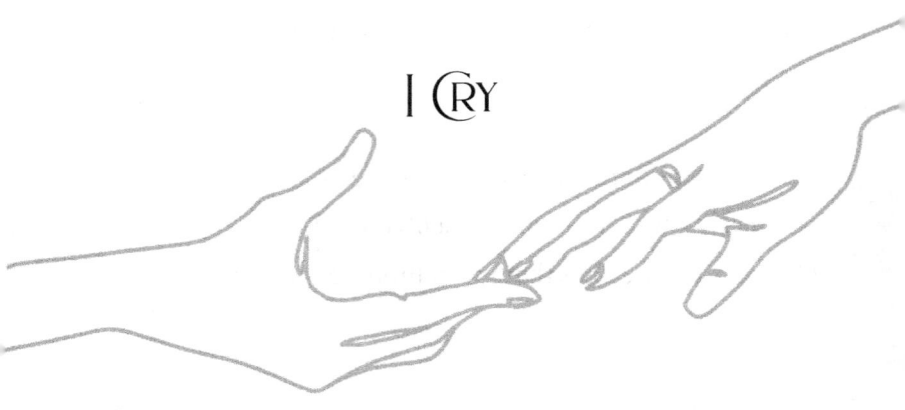

I Cry

I cry
Not for pain or sorrow
Not for grief or loss, I cry
Not for the shattering feeling of love lost,
But for the emptiness of forgetting the feeling of having ever loved.
For the desperate plea that wells up in my heart,
The incessant longing for feeling, for sensitivity…
For connection.

I cry because I'm one man on an island, stranded and left for dead

Forgotten by all, and all for the lack of connection.
I'm trapped in a cycle of drinks, drugs, and bad decisions
But don't judge until you've tasted from my cup...
After all, water and spirits look alike from a spectator's point of view.

I know I'm making the wrong choices
I know there's a right way to go,
And I know that I'm not going that way.
All for the albatross tied around my neck,
Dragging me clumsily down to hell
But what can I do when I have nothing left of my lifeline but a broken piece of string?

And what I wouldn't give to feel connected again, to one person or another, no matter the cost,
For I'd rather live my life with the pain of regret, knowing I loved and lost,
Than live out the rest of my days as numb as a lamp pole in deep winter.
I'd rather the pain of the cold than the numbness and lifelessness of no connection...

I'm not tired of being alive, I'm just tired of living without living, but I find comfort in the knowledge that the fight will soon be over, and I'll be able to finally rest in peace.

And as I prepare for my grave, I'm grateful for everything I've learnt and everyone I've met, I'm mostly glad that I'll finally be able to forget.

I Have Been Deceived

I have been deceived

I shan't believe the lies

I shan't believe the tales

I shan't believe it

The bull-crap that comes out of your mouth

The meaningless declarations of love

The false proclamations of affection

I have been deceived

I shan't ignore the truth

I shan't ignore the facts

I shan't ignore the reality

Of who I truly am to you
Of what I truly mean to you
Of where I truly belong in your heart

I have been deceived
I can't do this anymore
I can't take it anymore
I don't think I can survive this
I'd much rather believe the lies
Than face it and accept the truth
I really wish the lies were true

I have been deceived
I won't forget the memories
I won't forget the smiles
I won't forget the feeling
Of your lips pressed against mine
Of your body pressed against mine
Of your hands all over my body

I have been deceived
I can't let you go
I shan't let you go
I won't let you go
Though I refuse to believe the lies

Though I decide to accept the truth
I know I won't survive if I let you go.

I Wish

I wish I was filthy rich
I wish I was popular
I wish I was loved
I wish I had true friends

I wish my family loved me
For once, maybe they could understand
The pain I go through
Maybe they could help me
Maybe they could care

I wish I had a real friend

Someone to count on
To share my problems with
Someone to always help me
And talk away those lonely days

I wish I was brilliant
Though I know I already am
I wish I had more than that
To take me places
And make me someone now

I wish that I was rich
There, living my fantasy
Away from the real world
To a place of peace
To some sort of solitude

I wish you were still alive
You didn't have to die
At least, not now at least
You didn't need to go so soon
But trust, God has his reasons

I wish my life was better
Not as miserable as it is

I wish I had real friends like you
Not being me would be great
I would be free from the pain

I wish the world would stop turning
And people would have a heart
I wish that life would be good
That pain wasn't all I felt
And that, for once, people would show love

I wish I knew what it felt like to care
And how it felt to be cared for
And what it meant to love or be loved
And not hate or spite or regret
Or the hardest parts of life

I wish I were dead
Sometimes, maybe all the time
I wish I was away from this life
This life of misery and sorrow and hurt
This lugubrious state called life

I wish I was in heaven
In a state of grace and peace
Though, most times I don't deserve it

I just wish I could go there
To get away from the pain and heartbreak.

If Love Is A Crime

This funny feeling, I feel when I'm around you
Is unnatural to me
It is very strange to me

Sometimes I think I'm in love
Sometimes I'm not sure
Sometimes I want to be with you
Sometimes I'm scared to do so

If I'm in love with you
Then why is it so strange
Why do I feel so insecure

When I hear or speak your name?

Maybe it's wrong to fall in love
Or should I call it that
Does love really leave you so lost and perplexed
Or does it just help mesmerize?

Well, if this feeling is love
And this feeling is wrong
Then the feeling must be a real crime

Well, if love is a crime
Then I'm a fugitive of the law
For this feeling is lifelong.

I'm Learning To Love

As the wind blew softly, caressing my face, I realized how much I desired that soft touch. Just to feel wanted, just to feel needed, just to feel loved.

So, I'm learning to cherish the feel of the wind, the soft droplets of cool rain that stroke my hair, the warm rays of sunshine that kiss my lips.

I'm learning to cherish the sweet smell of freshly mown lawns and the look of fallen autumn leaves and, instead of letting them remind me of loved ones and good times, I'm learning to love these things.

The next caress upon my skin, the next kiss upon my lips, the next gentle, beautiful words whispered into my ear, they will remind me of the love and care nature has shown me, asking for nothing in return.

No catches, no clauses, just pure giving, pure loving which asks not even for my heart, but for me to be happy.

I'm learning to love the things that truly love me.

I'm Fine

I can't begin to count the number of times I've said "I'm fine"
"I'm alright"
When I'm clearly not.
But sometimes, it's harder to open up and let it out than to bottle it up and keep it in,
So I choose the easy way out, which is in
And in that moment realize that all I'll ever be is alone.
I feel tired

I feel tired
Like I want to sleep and not wake up

Like I want to fall from the 75th story
Just fall
I feel like I want to dangle from the tallest tree with the weight of my heart, head, and gravity helping the noose break my neck
I feel tired of thinking
Tired of breathing
Tired of being
I just want to disappear
To slowly fade away
To cease to exist
And I just feel tired
Tired of each sunrise and sunset ushering in a new cycle of 24s giving me 24 more reasons to die before 30
Tired of the sounds of the birds and the bees and the smell and feel of fresh air and warm sun on my skin
Cos all I feel is cold, bitter, empty tiredness

And yet I feel fine, cos fine means I'm still alive
Still awake
Still hoping to
Still wanting to
And yet not asleep
So, I'm fine

Just A Fact

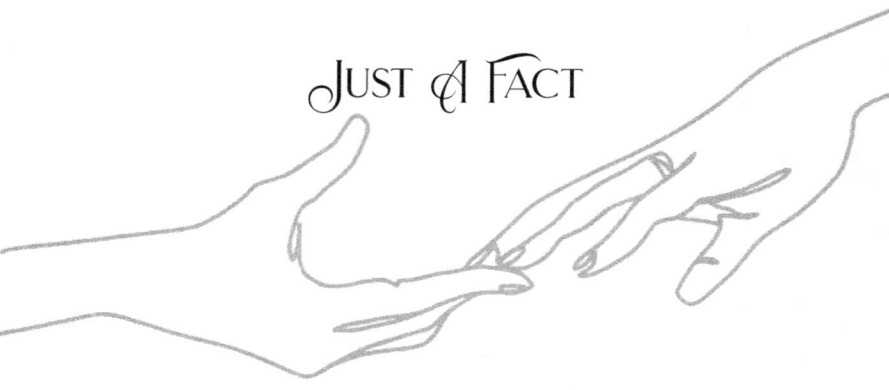

Life is painful

Being alive hurts

Breathing is a strenuous exercise

Thinking is an overly complicated process.

Sometimes I think it might be better to just end it all

And even that feels like more of a struggle than it's worth.

It's not a complaint, just a fact:

I'm tired of living.

My heart feels tired of beating

My lungs feel tired of breathing

My brain feels tired of thinking

My soul feels tired of feeling

And yet... I go on
Because feeling tired isn't a good enough reason to quit...
Though it's the best reason I've got... for now...
And so often I fear, if I were to find a better reason to quit, would I still keep living this life?
Even though my lungs beg for their last breath, would I still fight for one more?
Would I desire death? Or would I just carry on not wanting to be alive?

Maybe

Definitely, heartbreak isn't new
The solution is as painful as the cause
The thought of you makes me confused
Seriously confused

You know, if I had a choice,
I won't be the way I am right now.
You've made the difference in my life
So why do you get scared of me?

I watch the others follow you
You lead them like sheep follow a shepherd

I want to be different
But I wish to be part of the flock

I know it's not possible
But if only you knew the way I felt
If only you understood what I was going through
If only you could see

Then maybe you won't be so adamant
Maybe you'd give me a chance
Maybe you'd help me as a true friend
Maybe you'd feel the same way too.

Mumbo Jumbo

If we never had earth
Then we'd never have flown
If we did not have day
Then our dark times wouldn't be night

If we did not have the sound
We would not hear the silence
And if we did not have the dark
We would not see the light

If we did not live on land
Then we would not go swimming

If we did not grow our hair
Then it would not need trimming

If we do not sit, we cannot stand
And if we do not stand, we cannot sit
If we do not sleep, we cannot awaken
And if we do not awaken, we cannot sleep

All these are done
For the benefit of each other
So we should work together
To help one another

If you love someone, let them know
If they know, they may love you back
Look out for those who love you
And once you know them, love them back

I'm not sure of what I'm saying
And I'm not sure if it's making sense
But the sense brings fun to stupidity
And the stupidity brings fun to the sense

Some Days

Some days I sit and wish it will all come true
But if you don't get what you want,
What can you do?
A friend was my one wish, something I dreamt
I took it as a prophecy, one that I almost felt

It breaks my heart to know my misconception of this youth
And once again, I am obliged to believe the bitter truth

That friend was not the real friend
But better with one than none

Oh! The pain and all the anger I felt
When that one was gone

I just found out that if I want one, then I have to be of one's kind
So if you can't accept me for who I really am, then never mind.

Poetry In Motion

As I watch the beads of blood like sweat drip down my arms
I feel the pressure release
The end is near
This time, I do not hesitate.
My precision is on point, my tension steady
I press down hard and get ready to go.

The aim wasn't to die
It was to cease to exist
And even that, I couldn't do.

Puzzling Questions of The Heart

Why do people feel pain?
Why do they cry over a broken heart?
When they know it cannot be healed?
Why can't others feel your pain
Even when you try your best to express it?

Why do you ask and give but never receive?
Why don't you get what you want?
What do you do when you have to stand and watch all you've ever wanted given to someone who never wanted them?
What do you do when you give your heart

To someone who takes it and breaks it?
What do you do when you love everyone
And everyone loved everyone
Everyone except you?

What do you do when you find a friend?
Who builds up your hopes just to bring them crashing down again?
What do you do when the only one you love?
Is the only one who doesn't love you?

What do you do
When the only one who
Can stop you from crying
Is the one who made you cry?
Puzzling questions of the heart

Scars

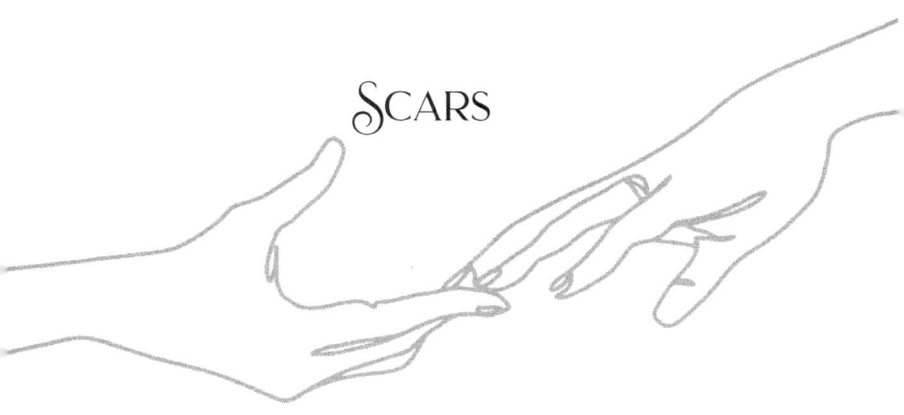

As steady as a beating drum, my heart beats in my chest...
Pumping blood rushing through my veins to the tips of my fingers and toes
And only God knows how hard it hurts to stay alive sometimes...

And when all is said and done, and everyone is gone,
I'm left alone to dance to the rhythm of my heart playing in my chest,
And I begin to move, mixing my salsa with my tears as I gasp for the breath of life for what I think could be my last time...

And as my head begins to sink, and as my eyelids slowly shut,
My gaze falls upon my chest...
And I see them...
Those scars...

Those scars I wear across my chest
From times I failed to be the best I could be,
From times people looked and couldn't see any good in me...
And they threw me aside as they took out the trash when they were spring cleaning out their lives...

Scars from times I loved so deep it carved a hole straight through my heart,
And it took days, and weeks, and months of surgery,
Lying under the blade of the Word setting asunder the cause of the incessant bleeding, as my heart beat faster,
A cupid's arrow lodged in my left auricle
Filling my veins with the poison I called love...
And it was killing me softly...

I honestly didn't know where to turn
Because everyone I went to seemed to think that

The only problem with my situation was me.
And as the daggers of "encouragement" pierced through my abdomen,
I realized it was harder to digest the truth
When the rest of the world thought you were the lie,
And lying there waiting for a Good Samaritan to hear my silent screams and help me to an inn,
Then I began to realize,
"Nobody knows who I really am…"
"Nobody can recognize me…"
"Nobody knows my name."

But somebody did…
And He picked me up…
And He cleaned me up…
And He called me by name…
Not liar or misfit… He knew my name.
And His voice was sweet as the nectar and smooth as honey…
And His hands were warm and gentle as He washed me clean with the water of His Word…
And His touch was so tender,
I didn't even feel the needle stitching me back together again…
And in His eyes was the beauty of sunrise and sunset,

Setting my fractures and mending my wounds
And by the time He was through, they were nothing but scars...
Those scars...

And I said, "Jesus, if you would heal me, why leave the scars? They only remind me of the hurt..."
I didn't understand then, you see...
Those scars...
The ones He left behind were not only to remind me of the hurt...

They were to remind me of the pain
And the times I hurt so bad
And the loneliness
And the anger
And the loss
And the rejection
And the times I was misunderstood...
And the people I trusted to be for me
Who went before me to hail me as the queen of the sinners and the condemned...
And I still hear their taunts...
And the names...

And I remember the feel of the earth as I lay dying,
With smoke in my eyes,
And the smell of the dust filling my lungs and the taste of my own blood in my mouth...
And you may wonder why I wear them so proudly...
And you remember me by the scars you gave me,
By the names you called me...
Like liar and loser, and weak and dysfunctional,
disobedient, a prostitute, disloyal, fake, unreliable, emotional...

And you look at them and see only flaws
That do not meet your standard of perfection...
Because they symbolize the hardships...
And failures and all the imperfections I embody.

These scars...
And as my shutting eyes fall upon these scars...
I feel it all again... And then I remember...
These scars are the trophies I carry from my battles.
They are the proof that I am more than a conqueror.
And you too will one day recognize me by the scars you gave me,
Because they remind me not only of what I've been through...

They remind me that I survived.

Selfish

When all is said and has been done

What's done is done,

And now begun to go then, when now was when we had we…

Now me…

No longer us but I

Not you but my once upon a time

Happily ever after singing

"… us against the world, you and me against them all…"

But when all is said and done

I see it's really the world against just me

Only me

But it's not only about me, I guess, that makes me selfish, protecting my heart
Which I offered up to you, body and soul, and found lying on the gravel-covered floor.

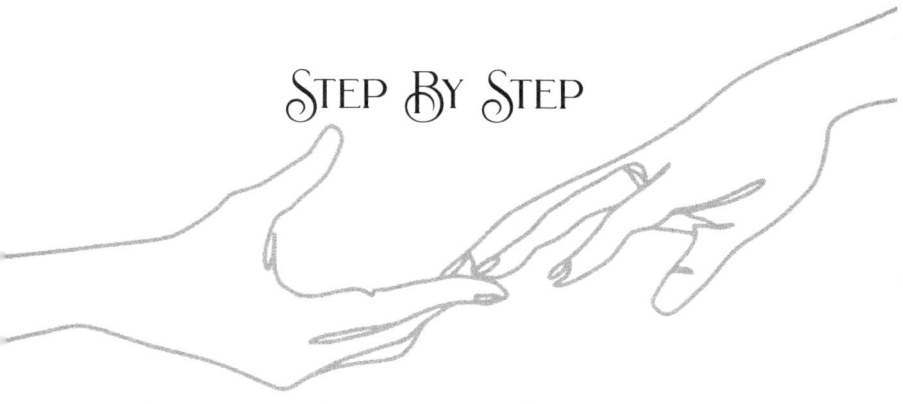

Step by Step

Step by step, we make our way, step by step
A child learns to walk
We all learn to talk
And to grow up like a tree
Sprouting from its seeds

Life is a path, it is a struggle
We make our way through
We push forward,
To grow, to learn, to lead
We try hard to learn to climb

To climb that mountain
To swim that sea
To walk that valley
To cross that desert
To reach the top

We struggle through life
We go through pain
Cross over hurdles
Endure certain sufferings
To make our way

Life is hard
I speak from experience
I wish it all to end
But I know I will make it someday
Step by step, I will make my way

Step by step

The Remedy

Juice dripping down my chin, I swallow a mouthful of sin
Its fruit, pleasing to my eyes. Its fruit, good for food
Its fruit, tasting so sweet in my mouth
As it slowly sinks down my throat and into my belly

I only took a bite, but just one bite was enough
I could feel the poison seeping into my system
Already filling my bloodstream with a slow, painful death
As it slowly sinks down my throat into my belly

One kiss, one touch, one night was enough

In a moment of weakness, in a turmoil of sheets
Resting in the strong arms of my savior
I traded my salvation for one bite of security

Not a fruit, or a tree... One bite of safety
Safety from my loneliness, safety from my insecurity
From the internal conflict of not being enough
Not slim enough, not smart enough, not good enough,

Not good enough for someone to want me
Not good enough for someone to love me
Not good enough for someone to choose me
Not good enough for someone to marry me

Me? not me, never me... What about me?
What was wrong with me? What had happened to me?
Why did it always have to be me?
Why did it always have to be about me?

With my eyes fixed only on me,
blurred hyper-myopia led me to find myself a savior
A knight in shining armor who would save me from me
I needed a hero, not some cross-hung, tombstone-rolling superstition

All I needed was one bite. Not a tree or a fruit
Just one bite would be enough to save me
Just one bite would be enough to change me
Just one bite would be enough to fix me

Just one bite was all I needed.
And I would give anything for that one bite
And he knew it. He could see my desperation
And he was not about to let this chance pass him by

Oh! what I wouldn't give for just one bite
I would trade my promise ring for one of rubber
My crowning glory to be just another number
Just another name on another man's list

As I signed my name out of the book of life
And into his list of exes, flings, and quick fixes
I had my hero right in the palm of my hand
And all I needed was just one bite

I knew it had to work, I knew it was the remedy
Nothing that costly would be that fake.
After all, I had sold my soul to save my senses
All I needed now was to take one bite.

I only took a bite, but just one bite was enough
I could feel the poison seeping into my system
Already filling my bloodstream with a slow, painful death.
And this death was the repugnant remedy he had mis-sold me.

Juice dripping down my chin, I swallow a mouthful of sin
Its fruit, pleasing to my eyes. It's fruit, good for food
Its fruit, tasting so sweet in my mouth
As it slowly sinks down my throat and into my belly

The Source

Why is my heart heavy?
Why is my soul scorched?
My body longs for the grave
My mind longs for peace

And though I can't explain it
I know in my heart the source of the pain
And it hurts so bad that I want to end it
To end it all completely

I don't have thirteen reasons why
I only have two

One is that you do not love me
And two, I can't stop loving you.

We alone know how much we cry in our closets
Dampened pillows alone bear testament to the pain within
Only we know what pain lies inside of us
Only we know what song our heart's sing

It is a melody like every other
One that rings with a silent key
As the deafening silence explodes eardrums
I wish, oh I wish…

I just wish he would love me for me.

Undeserved Gratification

Now the length of days grows short
And all the dreams I had are lost.
All the wishes I wish for myself, I wish for you also.

I pray for joy and peace in my life,
I hope for success
And look forward to a bright future

I am not wishing you this because you are special
Or because you deserve it,
But because I feel you should get it.

Because I feel you should be rewarded
For all you have done for me—
Nothing!

And for all the times you have made me cry,
Not by your deeds, but by your don't do's
And your ignorant and indifferent disposition towards me

I just want to say thank you.

Will Not Be Taught

Craft, creativity, my hands will learn

To paint and mould, and wield a pen

To express on keys, on drums, on strings

The melody many hearts will sing

My hands will not be taught to hold another's

My arms will not be taught to need another's

My eyes will not be taught to meet another's

My heart will not be taught to love another's

You And Me

Life is too short to wake up with regrets
So love the people who treat you right
Love the ones who don't, just because you can
Believe everything happens for a reason
If you get a second chance, grab it with both hands
If it changes your life, let it
Kiss slowly. Forgive quickly
God never said life would be easy
He just promised it would be worth it

Thank you for reading
These hands that hold the world
If you enjoyed this book, please consider leaving a review.

Also, check out ***A Kudzu Vine of Blood and Bone***, by Tristan Tuttle.

A Kudzu Vine of Blood and Bone
By Tristan Tuttle

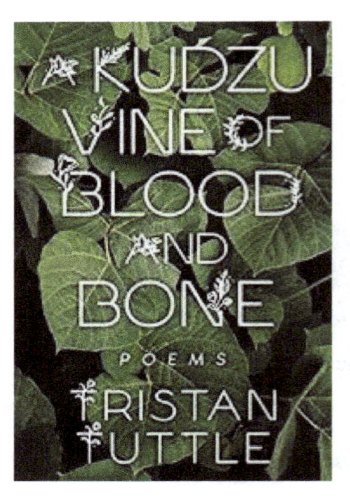

THERE'S A LOT TO BE said about kudzu. In the South, it's everywhere. You can't kill it. You can try, but you will drive yourself crazy. It's resilient. Just like me. Just like you. May we sprawl unflinchingly out of the dark corners of our lives and bloom.

A Kudzu Vine of Blood and Bone is Tristan Tuttle's debut poetry collection that takes the reader on a journey of self-discovery through motherhood, nature, and the spirituality that binds it all together. Weaving memoir into poetry, Tristan moves from quiet moments in the pine thickets to wild adventure in the Gulf of Mexico and discovers that "any dirt is fertile ground when you know what you're made of."

CPSIA information can be obtained
at www.ICGtesting.com
Printed in the USA
BVHW011101280822
645597BV00029B/1032/J